Enchanted *garden* crafts

susan cousineau

NORTH LIGHT BOOKS
CINCINNATI, OHIO

www.artistsnetwork.com

about the author

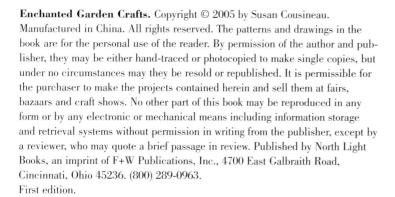

SUSAN COUSINEAU is a freelance designer and author living with her husband, Tom, and their very spoiled pets in the picturesque town of Fort Frances, Ontario.

In addition to Susan's first two books, *Easy Christmas Crafts* and *Spooky Halloween Crafts*, she has authored twelve previous booklets and has contributed to ten multidesigner books since the start of her professional design career over a decade ago. Several of Susan's designs have been published by national craft magazines and have appeared on numerous book and magazine covers. Susan has an honors degree in Business Administration and a diploma in Computer Graphic Design.

Susan hopes this book will inspire you to bring the beauty of nature into your heart and home all year long.

Enchanted Garden Crafts. Copyright © 2005 by Susan Cousineau. Manufactured in China. All rights reserved. The patterns and drawings in the book are for the personal use of the reader. By permission of the author and publisher, they may be either hand-traced or photocopied to make single copies, but under no circumstances may they be resold or republished. It is permissible for the purchaser to make the projects contained herein and sell them at fairs, bazaars and craft shows. No other part of this book may be reproduced in any form or by any electronic or mechanical means including information storage and retrieval systems without permission in writing from the publisher, except by a reviewer, who may quote a brief passage in review. Published by North Light Books, an imprint of F+W Publications, Inc., 4700 East Galbraith Road, Cincinnati, Ohio 45236. (800) 289-0963.
First edition.

09 08 07 06 05   5 4 3 2 1
Library of Congress Cataloging-in-Publication Data

Cousineau, Susan
    Enchanted garden crafts / by Susan Cousineau.
        p. cm.
    Includes index.
    ISBN 1-58180-449-0 (alk.paper)
    1. Handicraft. 2. Gardens in art. 3. Decorations and ornament--Plant Forms
I. Title.

TT157.C649 2005
745.5--dc22
                                        2004049206

Editor: David Oeters
Cover Designer: Marissa Bowers
Interior Designer: Karla Baker
Layout Artist: Amy Wilkin
Production Coordinator: Sara Dumford
Photographers: Christine Polomsky and Al Parrish
Photo Stylists: Mary Barnes Clark and Nora Martini

metric conversion chart

TO CONVERT	TO	MULTIPLY BY
Inches	Centimeters	2.54
Centimeters	Inches	0.4
Feet	Centimeters	30.5
Centimeters	Feet	0.03
Yards	Meters	0.9
Meters	Yards	1.1
Sq. Inches	Sq. Centimeters	6.45
Sq. Centimeters	Sq. Inches	0.16
Sq. Feet	Sq. Meters	0.09
Sq. Meters	Sq. Feet	10.8
Sq. Yards	Sq. Meters	0.8
Sq. Meters	Sq. Yards	1.2
Pounds	Kilograms	0.45
Kilograms	Pounds	2.2
Ounces	Grams	28.4
Grams	Ounces	0.04

welcome *spring!*

After a long winter's nap, it's always a joy to welcome the arrival of spring. Warm rays of sunshine fill the longer days as Jack Frost's icy splendor is magically transformed into glistening morning dew. The birds are singing, gardens are blooming and the flower fairies are celebrating the birth of a new season.

With *Enchanted Garden Crafts*, you'll blossom with creativity as you craft an exquisite collection of springtime-inspired gifts and garden delights. From a freshly picked bouquet of sweet treasures to enchanting garden décor, you're sure to find oodles of ideas to plant a medley of springtime fun in your home all year long.

May your heart be filled with sunshine and the magic of an everlasting garden as you celebrate the joy and beauty of spring!

Our dog, Jessie, celebrates the arrival of spring wearing a fragrant wreath of wildflowers. She loves to chase butterflies with her younger brother and sister, Jasper and Josie.

acknowledgments

As always, I offer a very special thanks to my family for their continued encouragement and support, especially my husband, Tom, Pops and Laurie, Auntie Mary, and Michael and Karen. And to our sweet Jessie, thanks for being such a "top dog" while posing for your featured photo.

I would also like to express my sincere appreciation to North Light Books for this exciting opportunity to share my garden creations, and to the very talented crew who worked so hard to make this book a reality: Tricia Waddell; my wonderful editor, David Oeters; Christine Polomsky and Al Parrish for your superb photos and Karla Baker for her fantastic book design. It is always a pleasure to work with such a great team!

My heartfelt thanks also goes out to all the companies who so generously provided the supplies for this book: Creative Paperclay Company (Michael Gerbasi), Delta Technical Coatings, Inc. (Barbara Carson), Loew-Cornell, Inc. (Shirley Miller), FloraCraft/DOW Styrofoam (Sharon Currier), Duncan Enterprises (Linda Bagby) and Activa Products, Inc. (Vickie Kay).

table of contents

lullaby garden · 10 ·

dream garden · 22 ·

garden gifts and greetings ·34·

garden party ·46·

tools & materials

This is an introduction to some of the basic supplies you will need to create the projects in this book. For a complete listing of the supplies required for each project, please refer to the individual project instructions.

brushes

Below is a list of the Loew-Cornell brushes used to create the projects in this book.

- American Painter Series 410: ⅛-inch (3mm), ¼-inch (6mm) and ⅜-inch (10mm) deerfoot stippler brushes
  Use the deerfoot stipplers to drybrush cheeks. The brush size will depend on the size of the cheek area for each project. These brushes are also used to drybrush ears and stipple fur texture. You can also use old "fluffy" brushes of various sizes for the dry-brush and stippling techniques.
- American Painter Series 4000: nos. 3 and 5 round brushes
- American Painter Series 4300: nos. 4, 6 and 8 shader (flat) brushes
- American Painter Series 4350: 10/0 and 0 liner brush
  Use the liner brush to paint fine details and delicate lines.
- American Painter Series 4550: ¾-inch (19mm) wash brush
  The wash brush is great for basecoating large areas.

general painting supplies

In addition to the brushes, you will need a few general painting materials.

- Delta Ceramcoat acrylic paints
  Refer to individual project instructions for suggested colors.
- Delta Ceramcoat crackle medium
- Delta Ceramcoat matte interior spray varnish
- Old toothbrush
  An old toothbrush is great for projects that use the spatter technique.
- Brush basin or water tub
  Rinse the brushes in a basin or tub during and after use.
- Paper towels
- Palette or waxed paper

PAINTBRUSHES

- Foam brushes
  Foam brushes are great for basecoating and applying crackle medium to large areas.

general supplies

Readily available supplies, such as the ones listed below, are sometimes not mentioned in the projects' materials lists, but should be kept on hand any time you are crafting. Skim through each project's instructions before you begin to make sure you have everything you need.

- Ruler
- Sharp scissors
- Wire cutters and pruners
- Sharp knife
- Hot glue gun and glue sticks
- Tacky glue
- Blow-dryer
  A blow-dryer speeds up the paint-drying process so you can get more done in your crafting time.
- Waxed paper
- Small pieces of sponge
  I use sheets of compressed sponges that expand in water, but any regular household sponge works fine.
- Fine point black permanent marker

transferring patterns

The following are materials you will need to transfer the patterns on pages 59-61. If you do not wish to transfer the patterns, use them as a guide and freehand the project details. For directions on transferring patterns and creating templates, see page 58.

- Transparent tracing paper
- Gray transfer paper
  You can use white transfer paper for projects that have dark backgrounds.
- Pencil and eraser
- Lightweight cardboard or posterboard
  Use cardboard or posterboard to make templates.

air-dry modeling clay

Creative Paperclay is a wonderful brand of air-dry clay that is extremely pliable and great for creating projects with a smooth, lightweight finish. It can be molded to create delightful characters such as the Wiggly Worm Favors and Ladybug and Bee Napkin Holders. The clay can be applied onto a Styrofoam base to create the enchanting Madame Butterfly and Flower Fairy Keepsake Box.

With a touch of springtime magic, the Paperclay can also transform an ordinary wooden spoon into a delightful garden fairy. It can also be flattened with a rolling pin, just like cookie dough. Once rolled, you can press your favorite cookie-cutter shapes into the flattened clay to make delightful ornaments for year-round decorating fun.

instant papier mâché

Celluclay Instant Papier Mâché is a great alternative to traditional papier mâché techniques. There are no strips of newspapers to cut or messy paste required. You simply mix the prepackaged paper pulp with warm water in a mixing bowl and you have an instant papier mâché mixture.

For these projects, the mâché mixture is applied onto Styrofoam ball and egg shapes. However, feel free to let your imagination run wild as you create all sorts of springtime papier mâché characters. A papier mâché covered Styrofoam egg makes the perfect garden frog, or use a variety of ball shapes to make a frightful family of insect critters. The possibilities are endless.

AIR-DRY MODELING CLAY

INSTANT PAPIER MÂCHÉ

modeling tips

- Cover your work surface with waxed paper or plastic wrap to prevent the clay from sticking.
- Keep excess clay in a resealable plastic bag to prevent dryness.
- For even drying, place the clay projects on a wire rack or grill to dry. Turn your projects over repeatedly to allow the air to circulate.
- Use a small heater or blow-dryer to speed up the drying process.
- Keep a bowl of warm water handy to clean and moisten your fingers. Use hand lotion to prevent dryness while sculpting your clay.
- Occasionally during the drying process, slight cracks may appear on the surface. Simply fill in the cracks with more clay and allow to dry.

painting terms & techniques

Below is a list of general painting terms and techniques used throughout this book. I've even included some tips to make your enchanted garden crafts even easier.

basecoating

Using a flat brush, apply at least two coats of paint to ensure solid coverage. Be sure to allow the paint to dry between coats. If you like, you can use a blow-dryer to speed up the drying process.

stippling

The stippling technique is great for creating fur texture. With a touch of paint on a deerfoot or old "fluffy" brush, gently pounce the bristles up and down to apply the desired texture.

drybrushing

For drybrushing, use a deerfoot brush or an old "fluffy" brush and dip the bristles in a small dab of paint. Remove most of the paint from the brush on a dry paper towel. You want the brush to be dry with just a hint of color. Gently rub the bristles on the surface area until you have achieved the desired effect. This technique is a great way to apply softly colored cheeks to your projects.

spattering

For this technique, use an old toothbrush to apply tiny specks of paint on the surface area. Although some crafters prefer to thin their paint with water first (approximately ⅔ paint to ⅓ water), I prefer to simply moisten the toothbrush bristles, then dip the toothbrush into a pool of paint. Remove excess paint onto a paper towel, then hold the toothbrush over the area to be spattered and run your finger across the ends of the bristles.

tip

If you apply too much paint during the stippling process, simply reverse or subdue the effect by stippling with the base color.

STIPPLING

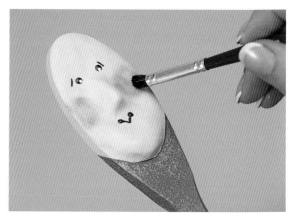

DRYBRUSHING

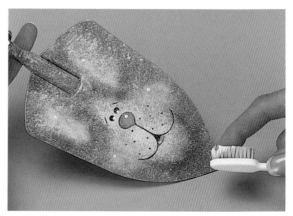

SPATTERING

wash

To create a wash, thin a small dab of paint with water to achieve a transparent color. Apply the wash to your surface, gradually adding more coats to deepen the color to the desired shade. This technique is commonly used to shade and antique projects.

dots and highlights

The easiest way to make dots is to dip the end of a paintbrush handle into a fresh dab of paint, then place the handle end onto your surface. Repeat this process for each dot. You can vary dot sizes by using a smaller or larger paintbrush handle. For tiny highlight dots, however, I recommend using the bristles of a liner brush.

sponge painting

Several projects have been painted using small pieces of sponge. I use sheets of compressed sponges that expand when moistened in water. To paint, you simply dip the dampened sponge into a pool of paint and apply it onto the surface of your project. It's important to remember that all painting should be done with a damp, not a wet, sponge. Be sure to squeeze the excess water from the sponge. If your sponge is too wet, the paint will bleed on your surface.

This sponge-painting technique can be used in many ways. For example, it can be used to apply a basecoat color to a project, create a textured effect or to add highlights. The size of the sponge you cut depends on the size of the area to be painted. When basecoating, you can apply additional coats as necessary to achieve solid coverage. Remember when cutting your sponge pieces they will expand slightly when moistened in water.

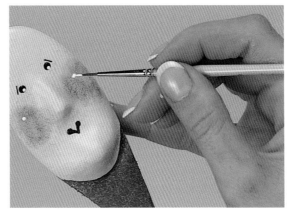

DOTS AND HIGHLIGHTS

painting tips

- Before attempting any new painting technique, always practice first on a scrap piece of paper.
- Cover your work surface with waxed paper. Waxed paper makes a cost-effective palette for your painting and sponge-painting techniques.
- Use a blow-dryer to speed up the drying process.
- Have a brush basin or container of clean water handy to rinse your brushes. Don't allow the paint to dry on your bristles.
- When you spatter, the more water you add to your paint or to the bristles of your toothbrush, the larger and more transparent the spatters will be.

lullaby garden

IN OUR LULLABY GARDEN you'll meet some delightful characters, who will no doubt capture your heart with their innocence and charm. You'll be buzzing with creativity when you craft a blossoming honey bear who can't wait to share his fresh-from-the-hive treat with his bumble bee friends. And you'll keep busy as a bee creating a gorgeous basket centerpiece from some woodsy garland and colorful garden trims. You'll also discover how easy it is to create a garden bunny topiary and glass ball bunny ornaments that will bring oodles of floppy-eared fun into your carrot patch.

And let's not forget those creepy-crawly critters that bring joy and laughter to kids of all ages. Our Lilly Ladybug and Bloomin' Bugs are guaranteed to do just that with their silly smiles. Or, if you prefer to add an entire bug collection to your garden décor, you can make our quick and easy Bug Catcher Bonnet in no time flat. Whether you're sweet on bunnies and bears or go "buggy" over our creepy-crawly friends, you're guaranteed to find your favorite garden lullaby to dream away those endless summer nights.

lilly ladybug

This lovable ladybug will warm your heart and home with her rosy red cheeks, red button nose and cheerful smile. Crafted from brown paper bags, this cute critter will add a charming touch of whimsy to your garden décor and make a wonderful project for kids as well.

materials

- Paintbrushes and general supplies (see pages 6–7)
- Kraft paper (such as heavy brown paper bags or parcel wrap)
- Tracing paper and transfer paper
- Lightweight cardboard or posterboard (optional: see page 58)
- Polyester fiberfill
- Delta Ceramcoat acrylic paint: Cardinal Red, Charcoal, Light Ivory and Fleshtone
- Delta Ceramcoat matte interior spray varnish
- Tulip Pearl Gold dimensional paint
- Two 12" (30cm) pieces of 20-gauge gold wire
- Two 7mm wiggly eyes
- ⁵⁄₁₆" (8mm) wooden button
- 19" (48cm) piece of miniature artificial leaf roping garland
- Six miniature artificial daisies (with stems removed)
- Five miniature wooden ladybugs
- 9" (23cm) piece of ⅛" (3mm) yellow ribbon
- Black fine point permanent marker

tip

If you plan to make several ladybugs, you can save time by transferring the pattern onto a piece of lightweight cardboard or posterboard. Once this cardboard template is cut out, you can use it over and over again to trace your pattern. See page 58 for tips on using patterns and templates.

1 Referring to the pattern on page 59, transfer the ladybug pattern twice onto kraft paper. Cut out the two ladybug shapes. Next, line up the edges of the two ladybug shapes and hot glue the inside edges together, leaving the head and shoulders open to stuff the fiberfill once the ladybug is painted.

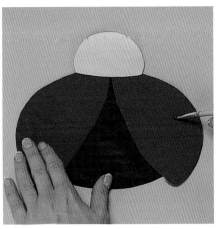

2 Referring to the pattern on page 59, basecoat the face with Fleshtone, the midsection with Charcoal and the wings of the ladybug with Cardinal Red.

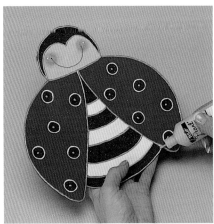

3 Paint the dots on the wings with Charcoal and outline with Light Ivory. Paint the three stripes on the midsection with Light Ivory and the top of the head with Charcoal. Drybrush the cheeks with Cardinal Red and use Light Ivory dots for the cheek highlights. When dry, line the mouth with the black marker. Use the Pearl Gold dimensional paint to outline the body, wings, stripes, neck, face and head, and add tiny dots to the center of the dots on the wings. Allow to dry. Paint the wooden button nose with Cardinal Red, and add a tiny Light Ivory highlight dot. Use an old, worn toothbrush to spatter the ladybug and wooden nose with Light Ivory. When dry, apply the matte spray varnish.

4 Use the tip of a paintbrush handle to stuff the ladybug with polyester fiberfill. As you work your way towards the upper half, glue the ends of the 19" (48cm) piece of leaf garland inside the shoulders for the hanger. For the antennas, twist each piece of wire into a coil shape. Continue stuffing towards the top of the ladybug. Hot glue the antennas inside the head, then glue the remaining edges closed.

5 Hot glue the eyes and the wooden button nose onto the ladybug's face. Cut a 9" (23cm) piece of the ⅛" (3mm) yellow ribbon. Tie a bow, then hot glue the bow onto the neck area. Hot glue a miniature daisy to the center of the bow. Hot glue the five miniature daisies and wooden ladybugs onto the leaf garland.

bumble bee bear

Everyone knows that bears love honey. . .

especially when it's fresh from the hive! Crafted

from instant papier mâché, this plump fellow shares

a sweet treat with his bumble bee friends.

materials

- Paintbrushes and general supplies (see pages 6–7)
- 4" (10cm) Styrofoam ball
- 2½" (6cm) Styrofoam ball
- Round wooden toothpick
- Instant papier mâché (I used Celluclay)
- White acrylic gesso
- Delta Ceramcoat acrylic paint: Golden Brown, Palomino Tan, Spice Brown, Charcoal, Light Ivory and Cardinal Red
- Delta Ceramcoat matte interior spray varnish
- Miniature straw beehive approximately 3" (8cm)
- Five 1" (3cm) black and yellow chenille bees
- Assorted white and yellow artificial flowers (I used white and yellow daisies with miniature white flower clusters for accent)
- Mixing bowl
- Measuring cup
- Black fine point permanent marker

tip

A miniature straw beehive makes a charming accent for your bear and can be found in the garden section of most craft stores. As a fun variation, you could also display your bear with a miniature clay pot painted to resemble a honey jar.

1 Using a sharp knife, cut a tiny sliver off the bottom of the 4" (10cm) Styrofoam ball so it stands upright without rolling over. Press the bottom of the 2½" (6cm) ball onto a hard surface to flatten it slightly. Insert a wooden toothpick halfway through the top center of the 4" (10cm) ball. Apply plenty of hot glue onto the area around the toothpick, then immediately press the bottom (flattened side) of the 2½" (6cm) ball through the toothpick to form the head. Allow the bear form to set.

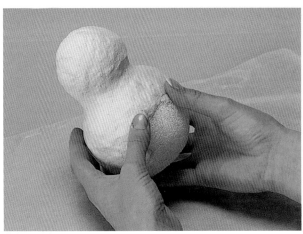

2 Mix the papier mâché with warm water in a mixing bowl, following the manufacturer's instructions. Using your hands, knead the mixture until it's smooth and has the consistency of stiff cookie dough. Cover your work surface with waxed paper. Use your fingers to apply the papier mâché mixture onto the bear form. Dip your fingers in a bowl of warm water to moisten, then blend the surface until smooth. If desired, allow the base form to dry before adding the features.

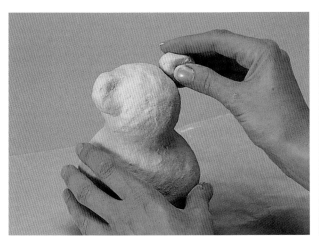

3 For the ears, form two 1" (3cm) balls of papier mâché. Press the balls firmly onto each side of the head, blending the edges until smooth. Indent the center front of the ears with your thumb.

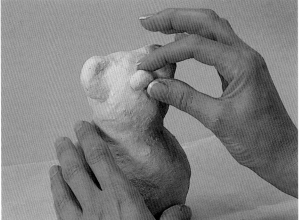

4 For the nose, form a ½" (1cm) ball of papier mâché. Press the nose onto the center of the face, blending the edges until smooth.

tip

If cracks appear in the papier mâché after drying, simply fill in with more papier mâché and allow it to dry again.

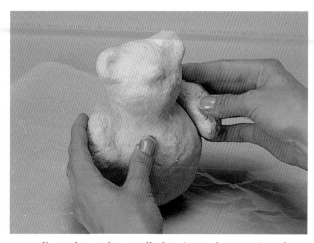 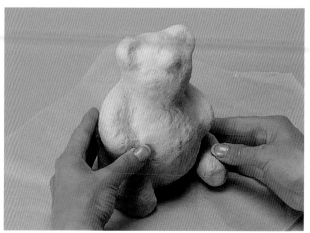

5 For each arm, form a roll of papier mâché approximately ¾" (2cm) wide and 2½" (6cm) long. Press each arm onto the side of the body, shaping as desired. Blend the edges until smooth. If necessary, add more papier mâché to build up the arm and shoulder area to achieve the desired shape.

6 For each leg, form a roll of papier mache approximately 1" (3cm) wide and 3" (8cm) long. Press each leg onto the bottom side of the body. Blend the edges until smooth. If necessary, add more papier mâché to build up the leg and hind quarter areas to achieve the desired shape. Place the bear on a wire rack or grill and allow to dry. When the bear is dry, apply a generous coat of white acrylic gesso to seal the surface of the bear form. When the gesso is dry, basecoat the bear with Golden Brown.

7 Refer to the face pattern on page 60. Paint the muzzle, bottom paws and inside the ears with Palomino Tan. Add highlights inside the ears with Light Ivory. Paint the nose with Charcoal and add a Light Ivory highlight dot. Paint the eyes Charcoal with Light Ivory pupils. For the cheeks, drybrush with Cardinal Red and place Light Ivory dots for highlights. Antique the bear with a wash of Spice Brown. When dry, outline the mouth and eyebrows and add the freckles with the fine point black permanent marker. Using an old, worn toothbrush, spatter the bear with Light Ivory. When dry, apply the matte spray varnish. Hot glue the floral trims onto the front of the bear and the top of the straw beehive. Hot glue three of the chenille bees onto the bear and the remaining two onto the beehive.

tip

If you draw the mouth, freckles and eyebrows with a fine point black permanent marker before you apply the antique wash, the marker may bleed onto the painted surface. If you prefer, you can add the mouth, freckles and eyebrows with Charcoal paint before you antique.

bloomin' bugs

Plant this merry trio of fluttering friends in your windowsill garden for a touch of springtime whimsy.

materials

- Paintbrushes and general supplies (see pages 6–7)
- Three 2½" (6cm) Styrofoam eggs
- Three 1½" (4cm) Styrofoam balls
- Three round wooden toothpicks
- Instant papier mâché (I used Celluclay)
- White acrylic gesso
- Delta Ceramcoat acrylic paint: Charcoal, Light Ivory, Fleshtone, Cardinal Red, Bright Yellow, Seminole Green
- Delta Ceramcoat matte interior spray varnish
- 6mm chenille stems: two 4" (10cm) black pieces for the ladybug, two 4" (10cm) black pieces for the bee, and two 4" (10cm) green pieces for the hornet
- ½" (1cm) buttons: two yellow for the bee, two red for the ladybug and two black for the hornet
- Three pairs of 4¾" (12cm) Fibre Craft nylon wings
- Three 2½" (6cm) rose pots (4" (10cm) high)
- Green sheet moss
- Artificial ivy foliage
- Assorted artificial floral trims in yellow and white
- Floral foam brick (cut to fit the rose pots)
- Metal garden rack approximately 13" (33cm) wide and 5" (13cm) deep
- Mixing bowl
- Measuring cup

1 For each bug, insert a wooden toothpick halfway through the small end of the 2½" (6cm) eggs. Apply hot glue around the toothpick then press the 1½" (4cm) ball through the toothpick. Allow the bug forms to set.

2 Curl one end of each chenille stem to form the antennas. Create two holes in the top of each head where the antennas will be inserted. Apply hot glue into the holes and insert the antennas.

3 Mix, then apply the papier mâché mixture onto the bug forms. Form the nose with a ⅜" (10mm) ball of papier mâché, then press and blend the nose onto each face.

4 When dry, apply gesso to the bug forms. When dry, basecoat all of the bug heads with Charcoal. Referring to the pattern on page 60, paint the faces Fleshtone and add Light Ivory eyes with Charcoal pupils. Paint the nose Charcoal with a Light Ivory highlight. Drybrush the cheeks with Cardinal Red and add highlight dots of Light Ivory. Outline the mouth, eyebrows and eyes using a liner brush and thinned Charcoal. Outline the neck area with Light Ivory.

- For the bee, basecoat the body with Bright Yellow. Paint the two stripes Charcoal and add Light Ivory dots.
- For the ladybug, basecoat the body with Cardinal Red. Paint the dots Charcoal.
- For the hornet, basecoat the body with Seminole Green. Paint the stripe Bright Yellow outlined with two Charcoal stripes. Paint the dots Light Ivory and outline with a thin Charcoal ring.

5 Using a toothbrush, spatter the three bugs with Light Ivory. When dry, apply the matte spray varnish.

6 Hot glue the buttons onto the antennas and the nylon wings onto the back of each bug.

7 Secure floral foam in each of the pots with hot glue. Glue green moss onto the floral foam, then hot glue the three bugs onto the mossy base.

8 Place the three bug pots inside the metal garden rack. Embellish the garden rack with the ivy foliage and the yellow and white floral trims.

garden bunny topiary

Hop into spring with this enchanting topiary bunny! He's "planted" in a clay pot and accented with moss, ivy and floral trims. Full of floppy-eared fun, this garden critter is simply charming with his twig whiskers and pink blossom nose. He's ready to guard your carrot patch with his fine feathered friend perched upon his ear.

materials

- General supplies (see page 6)
- 5" (13cm) clay pot
- 4" (10cm) Styrofoam ball
- 12" (30cm) piece of a ⅜" (10mm) wooden dowel
- Floral foam brick
- Two 11" (28cm) pieces of heavy general purpose wire
- Four 12" (30cm) square sheets of aluminum foil: cut each piece into three equal strips for a total of twelve 4"x12" (10cmx30cm) strips
- Green sheet moss
- 15" (38cm) piece of artificial ivy garland
- Facial trims: two artificial pink berries for the eyes, a 1" (3cm) pink flower for the nose, and six 2" (5cm) twigs for the whiskers
- 3" (8cm) mauve mushroom bird
- Five strands of natural raffia
- 12" (30cm) piece of ¼" (6mm) pink ribbon
- Assorted artificial pink and mauve floral trims with leaves and berries
- Pruners (for cutting the wire, dowel and twigs)

tip

For a charming variation of the project, instead of floral trims, you can accent the base of your bunny topiary with miniature artificial vegetables such as carrots, lettuce, tomatoes and onions. For a whimsical touch, you could also add vegetable seed packets or miniature garden tools.

1 Bend each general purpose wire piece in half to form an ear shape, then twist the ends of the wire to secure. Allow approximately 1½" (4cm) of twisted wire at the end of the ear shape to insert into the Styrofoam ball head. Wrap six aluminum foil pieces around each wire ear, leaving the twisted ends of the wire exposed.

2 Hot glue the wire ear shapes into the top of the 4" (10cm) Styrofoam ball. Use the dowel to create a 2" (5cm) deep hole in the bottom of the Styrofoam ball. Remove the dowel. Apply hot glue into the hole, then insert the dowel and allow the glue to set. Hot glue the green sheet moss onto the bunny head and ears.

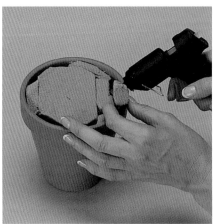

3 Use a sharp knife to cut the floral foam brick to fit the inside of the clay pot. Secure it in the pot with hot glue. Cut and glue smaller pieces of foam to fill in gaps around the base of the pot.

4 Create a 3" (8cm) deep hole in the center of the floral foam base with the dowel, then apply hot glue into the hole. Insert the dowel, with the moss head attached, into the hole. Hot glue moss around the wooden dowel and onto the base and front of the pot.

5 Hot glue the ivy garland and floral trims to accent the base and the dowel. Tie a raffia bow, then hot glue it to the dowel at the base of the bunny's head. Tie a bow with the pink ribbon, then trim it to the desired length. Hot glue the pink bow onto the center of the raffia bow.

6 Hot glue the two pink berries for the eyes and the pink flower for the nose. Hot glue the six twigs onto the face to create whiskers. Hot glue the rest of the artificial pink and mauve floral trims and berries onto the base of the pot. Finally, hot glue the mauve mushroom bird onto the top of the right ear.

busy bee basket

Our secret to making this super-easy project is using a packaged roll of grapevine garland. Its prerolled shape makes it a cinch to create a coiled "hive" base and circular handle in just a few simple steps. This "bee-utiful" basket is even sweeter than honey.

materials

- General supplies (see page 6)
- 15' (4.6m) package of rolled grapevine garland (approximately 1¼" (3cm) diameter)
- General purpose wire
- Two 3' (91cm) pieces and one 15" (38cm) piece of artificial ivy garland
- Straw beehive (approximately 3" (8cm) high)
- White and yellow floral trims (I use large artificial white shasta daisies, miniature artificial yellow daisies and small clusters of artificial cream bridal lace blossoms)
- Twelve 1" (3cm) chenille yellow and black bumble bees
- Two 24" (61cm) pieces of 1½"-wide (4cm) wired ribbon in yellow and green plaid
- Pruners or sharp scissors

1 Use a pair of pruners or sharp scissors to cut 3' (91cm) off the 15' (4.6m) grapevine garland. Wrap the ends of the garland pieces with wire to secure, and set the 3' (91cm) piece aside for the handle. Form the 12' (3.7m) piece of grapevine garland into a beehive shape, wrapping it higher in the center. Secure the shape with general purpose wire.

2 Using pieces of wire, attach the 3' (91cm) piece of garland onto each side of the beehive base for the handle.

3 Hot glue one 3' (91cm) piece of ivy garland around the basket and wrap the other 3' (91cm) piece around the handle. Hot glue the smaller 15" (38cm) piece of ivy garland around the top of the beehive shape.

4 Hot glue the straw beehive in the center of the basket, then add the floral trims. Hot glue the twelve chenille bees on the basket and straw beehive. Cut two 24" (61cm) pieces of the yellow and green wired ribbon. Tie each piece into a bow, then trim the ends to the desired length. Hot glue a bow onto each side of the handle.

Use wire to secure the shape of your Busy Bee Basket.

glass ball bunny ornament

materials: Paintbrushes and general supplies (see pages 6–7) • 2⅝" (7cm) glass ball ornament • Delta Ceramcoat acrylic paint: Lisa Pink, White, Charcoal and Metallic Kim Gold • Delta Ceramcoat matte interior spray varnish • Tulip Pearl Gold dimensional paint • Small piece of sponge • Green sheet moss • Floral trims: two miniature green leaves and a ¾" (2cm) pink paper rosebud • Two 2½" (6cm) pieces of 3mm pink pearl string • 8" (20cm) piece of ⅛"-wide (3mm) pink ribbon

1 Remove the ornament hanger. Using a dampened sponge, basecoat the glass ball with Lisa Pink. Apply two or three coats for solid coverage. When dry, very sparingly use the dampened sponge to apply Metallic Kim Gold for a textured effect. Let dry. **2** To paint the bunny, refer to the pattern on page 59. Basecoat the bunny shape with White. Paint the eyes Charcoal with White pupils. Paint the nose Lisa Pink with a White highlight dot. Drybrush the cheeks and inside of the ears with Lisa Pink. Paint the whiskers Charcoal. **3** Apply White dots randomly onto the surface of the ball. Let dry, then outline the bunny shape with the gold dimensional paint. Allow to dry. **4** Apply the matte spray varnish. When dry, reinsert the ornament hanger. **5** Hot glue the moss and floral trims onto the top of the ornament. Form a loop with the pink pearl strings and hot glue them behind the floral trims. Insert the ribbon piece through the ornament hanger and tie a knot at the end to secure. Hot glue the ribbon to secure it to the ornament.

bug catcher bonnet

materials: General supplies (see page 6) • 12" (30cm) straw hat • 22" (56cm) piece of green leaf garland • Florist wire or general purpose wire • Three artificial yellow roses • 26" (66cm) piece of 1½"-wide (4cm) yellow and green plaid wired ribbon • Miniature mesh screen bug catcher (approximately 5½" (14cm) long) • Miniature artificial bugs

1 Cut a 22" (56cm) piece of the green leaf garland. Form a circle with the garland, securing the ends with a small piece of wire. Hot glue the leaf garland around the brim of the straw hat. Be sure to position the garland so the wire piece will be at the bottom of the garland and concealed by the bow. **2** Hot glue the three yellow roses: one at the front and one on each side of the hat. **3** Tie a bow with the ribbon, then trim the ends to the desired length. Hot glue the bow to conceal the wired ends of the leaf garland. **4** Hot glue the artificial bugs around the brim of the hat as desired. Hot glue the mesh bug catcher onto the fabric bow. Accent the bug catcher with one or two of the smaller bugs.

dream *garden*

IF YOU FOLLOW THE SWEET AROMA of the wildflowers down
the wooded path, you'll discover a secret garden of wishes, daydreams and pure
storybook enchantment. And in the midst of your dreaming, you'll recapture the
childlike wonder of believing in the magic of fairies and angels as you craft your
own fairy-tale world of garden delights.

Look no further than your own kitchen cupboard to find the inspiration to
transform ordinary wooden spoons into enchanting garden fairies and those leftover
grocery bags into charming angel decorations. You can hide your secret wishes inside
a magical fairy keepsake box and create romantic birdhouse ornaments and dreamy
garden eggs.

If you truly believe in the magic of our Dream Garden, you might catch a glimpse
of our fluttering friend, Madame Butterfly, as she gathers the wild daisies that line
the edge of the garden path. Oh, what a special place to celebrate the many wonders
of spring!

flower fairy keepsake box

The freshly picked blossom on this box is actually a flower fairy in

disguise! Molded from a Styrofoam base and air-dry clay, she graces

a crackled keepsake box adorned with silk hydrangea blooms.

Perfect for storing your garden trinkets and treasures.

materials

- Paintbrushes and general supplies (see pages 6–7)
- 2½" (6cm) Styrofoam ball
- Air-dry modeling clay (I use Creative Paperclay)
- Round papier mâché box approximately 7" to 7½" wide (18cm to 19cm)
- Delta Ceramcoat acrylic paints: Seminole Green, Light Ivory, Maroon, Pale Yellow and Charcoal
- Delta Ceramcoat crackle medium
- Delta Ceramcoat matte interior spray varnish
- Tulip Pearl Gold dimensional paint
- 23" (58cm) piece of artificial leaf roping garland (to fit around the perimeter of the box)
- Two large artificial green leaves (approximately 4½" to 5" (11cm to 13cm) long)
- Ten artificial flowers in shades of ivory and soft yellow (five of each color)
- Black fine point permanent marker

tip

Tuck an assortment of flower seed packets into your fairy keepsake box for the perfect gift idea. For a touch of storybook whimsy, include a gift tag that reads: "Plant these magical seeds to attract flower fairies in your backyard."

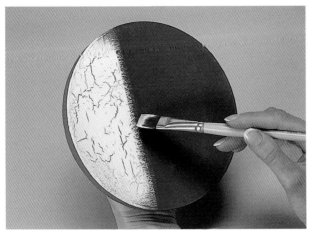

1 Basecoat the entire box and lid with Seminole Green. Allow to dry, then apply an even coat of crackle medium to the outer surface of the box and lid. Let the crackle medium air-dry until tacky, then apply a light, even top coat of the Light Ivory paint. Allow it to dry. The aged, crackle effect will appear within minutes. When dry, use an old toothbrush to spatter the outer crackled surface with Maroon and the inside green surface with Light Ivory. When dry, apply the matte spray varnish.

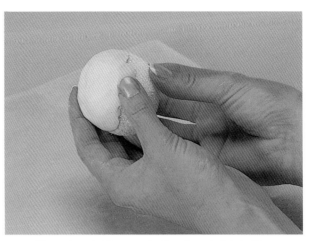

2 Use a sharp knife to cut the Styrofoam ball in half to form the base of the flower fairy's head. Cover your work surface with waxed paper. Apply the air-dry modeling clay onto the surface of the Styrofoam base. Blend the surface with moistened fingers until smooth.

3 For the petals, form eight 1" (3cm) balls of clay. Indent the center of each ball with your thumb for shape and definition. Press the petals firmly along the outer edge of the head until secure. Blend the edges and between each petal with moist fingers until smooth. Turn the fairy head over and continue to smooth and blend the petals together, using more pieces of clay as necessary to secure.

tip

Avoid the urge to overbrush the top coat on your crackle medium or you will smear the paint.

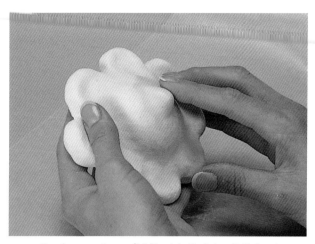

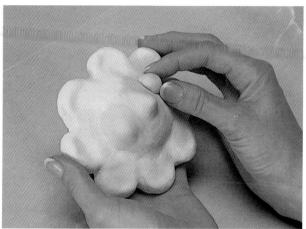

4 For the nose, form a ½" (1cm) ball of clay. Roll the clay into a nose shape, then press it onto the center of the face. Blend the edges of the nose until smooth.

5 Form two ½" (1cm) balls of clay. Press the two balls onto each side of the nose for cheeks. Blend the edges until smooth. Allow the clay flower fairy to dry. Note: If slight cracks appear after drying, fill them in with more clay and allow to dry.

6 To paint the flower fairy, refer to the pattern on page 59. Basecoat the face Pale Yellow and the petals Maroon. Paint the eyes Charcoal with Light Ivory pupils. Paint the lips Maroon and add a Light Ivory highlight. Drybrush the cheeks, with Maroon, and add a highlight dot with Light Ivory. Paint the dots on the petals with Light Ivory. Outline the mouth and eyebrows with the fine point black permanent marker. Paint dots at the end of the mouth with Charcoal. Use the Pearl Gold dimensional paint to outline the outer edge of the face and to apply a highlight stroke to each petal. Allow to dry, then spatter the flower fairy with Light Ivory using an old, worn toothbrush. When dry, apply the matte spray varnish.

7 Hot glue the two leaves onto the lid of the box for the fairy wings, then hot glue the clay flower fairy face onto the center of the wings. Hot glue the ten artificial flowers around the edge of the lid, alternating with the smaller yellow and the larger ivory flowers. Hot glue a piece of garland around the base of the box.

madame butterfly

As keeper of the garden, Madame Butterfly watches over her fragrant blooms as she flutters faintly overhead. With her charming clay pot body and whimsical clay face, she spreads springtime cheer to young and old alike, and is a welcome addition to any garden.

materials

- Paintbrushes and general supplies (see pages 6–7)
- 4" (10cm) rose pot
- 3" (8cm) Styrofoam ball
- Air-dry modeling clay (I use Creative Paperclay)
- Two 14" (36cm) pieces of 20-gauge gold wire
- Delta Ceramcoat acrylic paint: Seminole Green, Pale Yellow, Light Ivory, Maroon and Charcoal
- Delta Ceramcoat matte interior spray varnish
- Tulip Pearl Gold dimensional paint
- Two pairs of Darice 4¾" (12cm) nylon angel wings
- 10" (25cm) piece of ⅜"-wide (10mm) gold ribbon
- Six artificial green leaves (approximately 1½" to 2" (4cm to 5cm))
- One artificial white daisy and three miniature yellow flowers
- Black fine point permanent marker

1 Cut a small sliver off the bottom of the 3" (8cm) Styrofoam ball so it stands upright. Apply the air-dry modeling clay onto the surface of the Styrofoam ball.

2 For the nose, form a ½" (1cm) ball of clay. Roll the clay into a nose shape, then press it onto the center of the face. Form two ½" (1cm) balls of clay. Press the balls onto each side of the nose for cheeks. Blend the edges of the nose and cheeks until smooth.

3 Bend each 14" (36cm) wire piece into a coil shape and insert them into the top of the head for antennas. Remove the antennas and allow the clay head to dry.

4 To paint Madame Butterfly, refer to the pattern on page 59. Basecoat the head with Pale Yellow and the face with Light Ivory. Paint the eyes with Charcoal and add Light Ivory pupils. Paint the lips Maroon with a Light Ivory highlight. Drybrush the cheeks with Maroon and add a highlight dot to each cheek with Light Ivory. Outline the mouth and eyebrows with the black fine point permanent marker. Paint the dots at the end of the mouth with Charcoal. Use the Pearl Gold dimensional paint to outline the outer edge of the face and to apply the dot pattern. Allow to dry, then spatter the head with Light Ivory using an old, worn toothbrush. When dry, apply the matte spray varnish.

5 Insert the antennas back into their holes with tacky glue. Let the glue set.

6 Basecoat the clay pot Seminole Green with a Pale Yellow vertical midsection. The stripes are Light Ivory. Use the Pearl Gold dimensional paint to outline the midsection and the stripes and to add the dot pattern on the green painted area. Allow to dry, then spatter the clay pot body with Light Ivory using an old, worn toothbrush. When dry, apply the matte spray varnish.

7 Hot glue the butterfly head onto the clay pot and the two pair of wings onto the back of the clay pot.

8 Tie a bow with the 10" (25cm) piece of gold ribbon. Hot glue the bow onto the neck area, and the leaves and flowers onto the front center of the clay pot body.

paper bag garden angel

Crafted from brown paper bags, this heavenly garden angel keeps careful watch over her fluttering friends. With her gold-leaf wings and delicate floral accents, this dreamy delight brings the peace and serenity of an enchanted garden into your home all year long.

materials

- Paintbrushes and general supplies (see pages 6–7)
- Small piece of sponge
- Kraft paper (such as heavy brown paper bags or parcel wrap)
- Tracing paper and transfer paper
- Lightweight cardboard or posterboard (optional: see page 58)
- Polyester fiberfill
- Delta Ceramcoat acrylic paint: Seminole Green, Maroon, Light Ivory, Fleshtone and Metallic Kim Gold
- Delta Ceramcoat matte interior spray varnish
- 14" (36cm) piece of miniature artificial leaf roping garland (for hanger)
- 9" (23cm) piece of ⅛"-wide (3mm) gold ribbon
- Three gold-accented green leaves, approximately 2½" (6cm)
- Artificial white hydrangea flower (with stem removed)
- Green sheet moss
- Miniature artificial yellow flower and two small sprigs of cream bridal lace
- Two gold leaves approximately 3" (8cm) or green leaves painted with Metallic Kim Gold
- 1½" (4cm) miniature bird's nest
- Three ½" (1cm) miniature plastic speckled eggs
- 1¼" (3cm) miniature green and yellow bird
- Two 2¾" (7cm) artificial yellow butterflies
- 6" (15cm) miniature garden rake
- Miniature plastic dragonfly approximately 1" x 1¼" (2cm x 3cm)
- Black fine point permanent marker

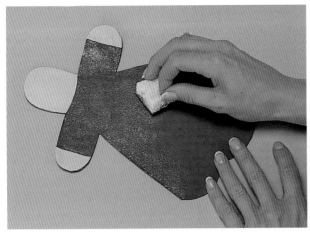

1. Use the pattern on page 60 to trace and cut out two angel shapes from kraft paper. Line up the edges of the angel shapes and hot glue the inside edges together, beginning at the top of the head and moving about halfway down each side to include the arms. Leave the bottom of the dress open to stuff fiberfill. Basecoat the face and hands with Fleshtone. Basecoat the dress with Seminole Green. When dry, use a small piece of dampened sponge to apply Metallic Kim Gold onto the dress for a textured effect.

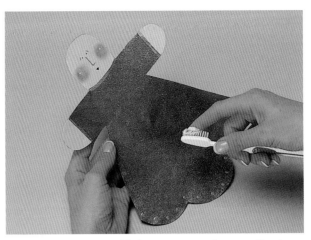

2. Use the fine point black permanent marker to outline the eyes, nose and eyebrows. Paint the mouth Maroon. For the cheeks, drybrush with Maroon and add tiny Light Ivory dots for cheek highlights. Use Metallic Kim Gold for the trim on the sleeves and collar and for the dots on the bottom of the dress. Then spatter the angel with Light Ivory using an old, worn toothbrush. When dry, apply the matte spray varnish.

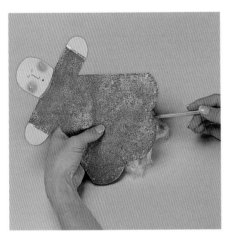

3. Use the tip of a paintbrush handle to stuff the head and arms with small pieces of polyester fiberfill. Continue working your way towards the bottom, adding more fiberfill as you glue the remaining inside edges shut.

4. Hot glue small pieces of green sheet moss onto the top of the head for hair. Glue the miniature yellow flower and cream bridal lace sprigs to accent the mossy hair. Hot glue the two gold leaves onto the back of the angel for the wings, and the 14" (36cm) piece of leaf garland onto the back of the angel for the hanger.

5. Tie a bow with the gold ribbon. Hot glue the bow onto the neck, the three gold-accented green leaves and the hydrangea flower on the dress, and a butterfly just below. Hot glue the other butterfly to the bottom left side of the garland, and hot glue the rake onto the left side of the angel. Glue the dragonfly onto the rake. Glue the three eggs inside the bird's nest. Glue the nest and the bird on the right side of the angel.

spoon fairies

With a sprinkling of storybook magic, you can transform ordinary wooden spoons into enchanting garden fairies. With their molded clay faces, iridescent wings and charming garden trims, these mystical delights are sure to spread springtime joy into your fairy-tale world.

materials

- Paintbrushes and general supplies (see pages 6–7)
- Wooden spoons in various sizes
- Air-dry modeling clay (I use Creative Paperclay)
- Delta Ceramcoat acrylic paint: Fleshtone, Seminole Green, Maroon, Charcoal, Light Ivory and Metallic Kim Gold
- Delta Ceramcoat matte interior spray varnish
- Small pieces of sponge
- Green sheet moss
- Darice 4¾" (12cm) nylon angel wings
- Miniature artificial leaf or floral roping garland (a 6" (15cm) piece to accent the top of each head plus a piece to wrap around the handle of the spoon)
- 9" (23cm) piece of ⅛"-wide (3mm) gold ribbon
- 22" (56cm) piece of 20-gauge gold wire
- ⅜" (10mm) wooden dowel (to curl the wire hanger)
- Mauve and green artificial berry sprigs
- Assorted garden trims, such as miniature birds, bees, frogs, dragonflies and butterflies

tip

Fibre Craft also makes 4¾" (12cm) nylon angel wings. However, each manufacturer's measurement relates to a different dimension. Therefore, the sizes of wings between companies are much different. Check the size of the wings for your Spoon Fairy before purchasing.

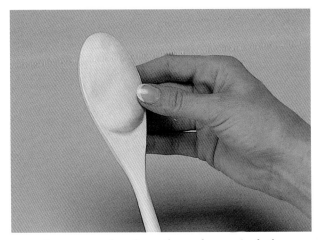

1 Cover your work surface with waxed paper. Apply the air-dry modeling clay onto the large curved end of the wooden spoon to form the face. Blend the surface with moistened fingers until smooth.

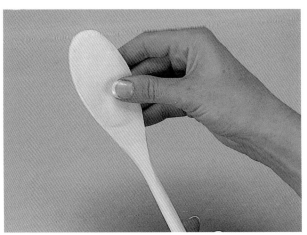

2 Form a ½" (1cm) ball of clay. Press the ball onto the bottom of the clay face, and using your fingers, blend the edges to form a chin shape. If necessary, add more clay to achieve the desired shape. Blend the chin onto the face until smooth.

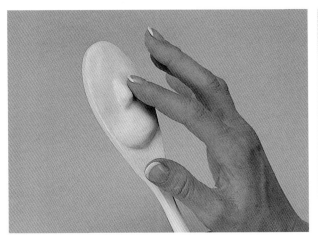

3 For the nose, form a ⅜" (10mm) ball of clay. Roll the clay into a nose shape, then press it onto the center of the face. Blend the edges of the nose until smooth. Allow the clay to dry.

4 To paint the spoon fairy, refer to the pattern on page 61. Basecoat the face with Fleshtone and the handle of the spoon with Seminole Green. When dry, use a small piece of dampened sponge to apply Metallic Kim Gold onto the handle for a textured effect.

tip

Moisten your fingers with water to make blending easier. Use hand lotion to prevent dryness while sculpting with clay.

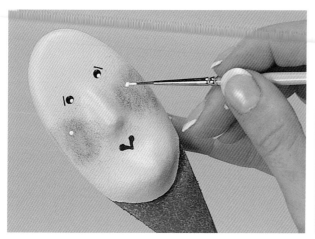

5 Paint the eyes Charcoal and add Light Ivory pupils. The eyebrows are Charcoal. The mouth is Maroon. For the cheeks, drybrush with Maroon, then add a highlight dot onto each cheek with Light Ivory. Apply the matte spray varnish when the paint is dry.

6 Hot glue small pieces of green moss around the front and onto the back of the head for the hair. Glue the 6" (15cm) garland around the top of the head. Hot glue more garland around the handle of the wooden spoon. Glue the artificial berry sprigs onto the top of the head. Tie a bow with the gold ribbon and trim the ends, then glue the bow under the chin of the spoon fairy. Finally, glue garden trims, such as miniature birds, bees, frogs, dragonflies and butterflies, onto the fairy.

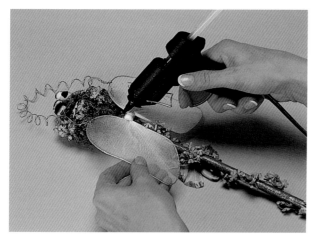

7 Curl the 22" (56cm) piece of gold wire around the wooden dowel. To create a hanger, insert the ends of the gold wire into the top of each wing, then twist the ends to secure the wire. Hot glue the wings onto the back of the wooden spoon. Add more miniature garden trims to the wings if you desire.

tip

For a magical touch, purchase the wings with iridescent glitter. They'll look like they've been sprinkled with glistening fairy dust. Or, you can spray plain wings with the matte spray varnish, then sprinkle them with fine iridescent glitter.

birdhouse ornaments

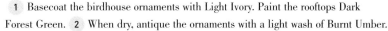

materials: General supplies (see page 6) • Miniature papier mâché birdhouse ornaments [approximately 2½" to 3" (6cm to 8cm)] • Delta Ceramcoat acrylic paint: Light Ivory, Dark Forest Green and Burnt Umber • Delta Ceramcoat matte interior spray varnish • 8" (20cm) piece of ⅛"-wide (3mm) pink or mauve ribbon (for each ornament) • Floral trims

1 Basecoat the birdhouse ornaments with Light Ivory. Paint the rooftops Dark Forest Green. **2** When dry, antique the ornaments with a light wash of Burnt Umber. **3** Using an old, worn toothbrush, spatter the ornaments with Burnt Umber then Light Ivory. When dry, apply the matte spray varnish. **4** Hot glue the floral trims onto the birdhouse ornaments as desired. **5** Tie a bow with the 8" (20cm) piece of the ⅛" (3mm) pink or mauve ribbon, then trim the ends to the desired length. Hot glue the bow onto the floral trims.

romantic garden eggs

materials: General supplies (see pages 6) • Papier mâché eggs [I use one 6" (15cm) and two 5" (13cm)] • Delta Ceramcoat acrylic paint: Light Ivory and Burnt Umber • Delta Ceramcoat matte interior spray varnish • Natural raffia (five or six strands for each egg) • Floral trims [I use small artificial ivy sprigs, miniature pink paper rosebuds and mauve berry clusters) • 2" (5cm) pink or mauve bird

1 Basecoat the papier mâché eggs with Light Ivory. **2** When the paint is dry, antique the eggs with a light wash of Burnt Umber. **3** Using an old, worn toothbrush, spatter the eggs with Burnt Umber. Apply the matte spray varnish when the paint is dry. **4** For each egg, tie five or six strands of natural raffia together with a smaller piece of raffia (in the center) to form a single cluster. Tie the raffia clusters around the center of each egg. Trim the ends to the desired length, and secure the raffia with hot glue. **5** Hot glue the ivy sprigs, paper rosebuds and berry clusters onto the raffia trim. Glue a 2" (5cm) pink or mauve bird onto the larger egg.

garden gifts and greetings

THE GARDEN IS LIKE A BREATH of fresh air. It is a wondrous source of inspiration for creating gorgeous gifts and decorative delights to warm the hearts of family and friends. And there's no better way to share a sunny garden welcome than with our enchanting Garden Greetings Wreath blooming on your front door. Accented with romantic floral trims and a bevy of garden delights, this exquisite grapevine decoration celebrates the promise of spring all year long.

Our garden-inspired gift ideas will spread the endless beauty and simple joys of the season to those close to your heart. Brighten a special friend's day with a pair of Friendship Garden Gloves or send a Cup of Cheer as a thoughtful get-well sentiment. Transform an inexpensive garden spade into a charming Bunny Spade and a blank memory book into a romantic Keepsake Journal.

Coordinate your garden gifts with an exquisite handmade card crafted from a paper doily and delicate floral trims. You can create keepsake cards that are beautiful enough to showcase. And as you're crafting your gifts and greetings, always remember that no matter what the occasion, a gift of garden joy and enchantment is always in season.

bunny spade

Who says gardening tools are just for planting? With a few painting supplies, you can transform an inexpensive garden spade into a blooming bunny decoration. Accented with floral trims and a raffia bow, this cute critter will surely hop his way into your heart and home.

materials

- Paintbrushes and general supplies (see pages 6–7)
- Garden spade with metal blade and a hole in the handle
- Delta Ceramcoat acrylic paint: Quaker Grey, Raw Sienna, Light Ivory, Burnt Umber and Lisa Pink
- Delta Ceramcoat matte interior spray varnish
- Assorted artificial floral trims in pink and mauve
- Three strands natural raffia
- ¼"-wide (6mm) pink ribbon [10" (25cm) piece for the bow and a 12" (30cm) piece for the hanger]
- Artificial pink or mauve butterfly [approximately 2" to 2½" (5cm to 6cm)]

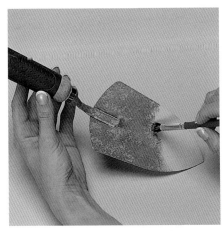

1 To paint the bunny spade, refer to the pattern on page 61. Basecoat the metal blade with Quaker Grey. Using the ⅜" (10mm) deerfoot brush, or an old "fluffy" brush, stipple the blade with Raw Sienna, allowing just a touch of the grey background to show through.

2 Very sparingly, stipple the blade with Light Ivory to softly highlight and add texture. Then stipple more heavily with Light Ivory to paint the face and inside of the ears.

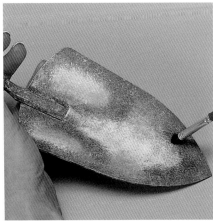

3 Drybrush the cheeks and inside of the ears softly with Lisa Pink. Very sparingly, stipple the outer edge of the face and ears with Burnt Umber to softly shade and add dimension.

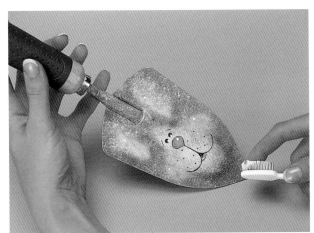

4 Use the pattern on page 61 to transfer the facial features onto the blade. Then paint the bunny. Paint the eyes Burnt Umber with Light Ivory pupils. Paint the eyebrows with a thin line of Burnt Umber. The nose is a mixture of Lisa Pink and Raw Sienna. Shade the outer edge of the nose with Raw Sienna. Outline the nose and mouth with a liner brush and thinned Burnt Umber. Add a highlight dot of Light Ivory to the nose. Paint the freckles with tiny Burnt Umber dots. Paint the lips with a mixture of Lisa Pink and Raw Sienna. Add a highlight stroke of Light Ivory to the lips and Light Ivory highlight dots to the ears and cheeks. Finally, use a toothbrush to spatter the blade with Light Ivory. When dry, apply the matte spray varnish.

5 Insert the 12" (30cm) piece of the pink ribbon through the hole of the handle. Tie a knot to secure, then hot glue the knotted end of the ribbon behind the handle. Tie a bow using three strands of natural raffia, and hot glue it to the base of the handle. Tie the 10" (25cm) piece of the pink ribbon in a bow, and hot glue it to the center of the raffia bow. Glue the floral trims onto the handle, and glue the butterfly onto the floral trims.

garden greetings wreath

Bring the enchantment of a quaint country garden into your home with this glorious grapevine wreath. Accented with romantic rose blossoms and a bevy of gardening delights, this exquisite creation will spread springtime cheer to young and old alike.

materials

- Paintbrushes and general supplies (see page 6)
- 14" (36cm) grapevine wreath
- Delta Ceramcoat acrylic paint: Spice Brown and Light Ivory
- Delta Ceramcoat matte interior spray varnish
- Delta Ceramcoat crackle medium
- Wooden garden gate fence embellishment [7½" (19cm) wide by 4¾" (12cm) high]
- Wooden sign [5½" (14cm) wide and 2¼" (6cm) high]
- Garden-style alphabet stickers (I use Provo Craft Pathways stickers)
- 80" (203cm) of an artificial green leaf or ivy garland
- Green sheet moss
- Three clusters of artificial flowers with leaves and berries
- Three 1" x 1¼" (2cm x 3cm) miniature clay pots
- 3" (8cm) straw hat
- Two artificial miniature leaves and a berry sprig (for the hat)
- 6½" (17cm) miniature shovel
- Miniature artificial insects (I use one dragonfly, three grasshoppers, one butterfly and two bumble bees)
- Miniature silk vegetables

tip

You can find floral candle rings and cut them apart into the three sections to create the clusters of artificial flowers.

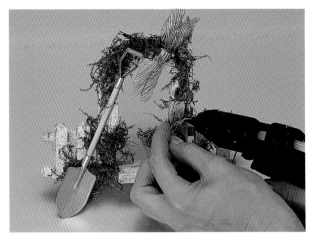

1   Basecoat the fence with Spice Brown. Allow it to dry, then apply an even coat of the crackle medium. Let the crackle medium air-dry until tacky, then apply a light, even top-coat of the Light Ivory paint. Allow it to dry. You will notice the aged, crackle effect within minutes. Spatter the fence with Spice Brown using an old, worn toothbrush. When dry, apply the matte spray varnish. Finally, glue pieces of green moss to the fence. Then glue the shovel, dragonfly and one of the clay pots. Add small pieces of moss inside the clay pot.

2   Follow step 1 to paint the sign. Apply the alphabet stickers onto the sign to spell "Garden Greetings." Glue pieces of green sheet moss around the sign. Then glue the butterfly and one of the grasshoppers onto the sign.

3   Wrap the garland around the wreath and hot glue it to secure.

4   Hot glue the decorated fence to the bottom of the wreath and the sign to the top of the wreath.

5   Referring to the photo for placement, hot glue the three clusters of artificial flowers and the miniature silk vegetables onto the wreath. Glue moss inside the remaining two clay pots, then glue both pots to the wreath. Glue small pieces of moss, leaves and the berry sprig onto the brim of the straw hat, and glue the hat onto the wreath. Finally, glue the bumble bees and grasshoppers onto the wreath.

decorated garden fence

This charming garden scene takes us back to the summers of long ago. We would spend our carefree afternoons daydreaming, picking wildflowers and strolling through the meadow. With just a few easy steps, you can transform a miniature wooden fence into a decorating delight that recaptures the summertime joy and enchantment of years past. What a delightful way to relive those lazy days of summer.

materials

- Paintbrushes and general supplies (see page 6)
- Wooden garden fence [9" (23cm) wide and 4¼" (11cm) high]
- Delta Ceramcoat acrylic paint: Spice Brown, Light Ivory, Dark Forest Green and Georgia Clay
- Delta Ceramcoat crackle medium
- Delta Ceramcoat matte interior spray varnish
- Green sheet moss
- Miniature wooden birdhouse [approximately 1¾" (4cm)]
- 36" (91cm) piece of 20-gauge gold wire
- ⅜" (10mm) wooden dowel (to curl wire hanger)
- Three miniature artificial ivy sprigs
- Assorted miniature artificial flowers in white and yellow (with stems removed)
- 1½" (4cm) miniature bird's nest
- Three ½" (1cm) plastic speckled eggs
- Two 1¼" (3cm) miniature green and yellow birds
- Miniature shovel [approximately 6½" (17cm) long]
- 2" (5cm) miniature grapevine wreath
- 1½" (4cm) split wooden flowerpot
- Three strands of natural raffia
- Drill and ¹⁄₁₆" (2mm) drill bit

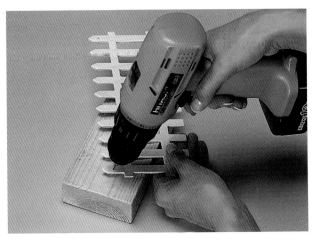

1 Using the ¹⁄₁₆" (2mm) bit, drill a tiny hole in the top of the left and right sides of the fence.

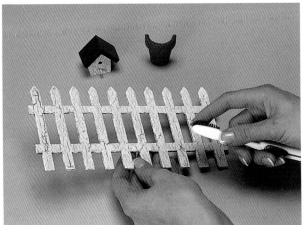

2 Basecoat the fence with Spice Brown. Allow to dry. Apply an even coat of the crackle medium onto the fence. Let the crackle medium air-dry until tacky. Apply a light, even topcoat of the Light Ivory paint. When dry, spatter the fence with Spice Brown using an old, worn toothbrush. Repeat the same painting steps for the base of the miniature birdhouse. Paint the roof with Dark Forest Green. Spatter with Spice Brown. Paint the wooden flowerpot with Georgia Clay. When all the pieces are dry, apply the matte spray varnish.

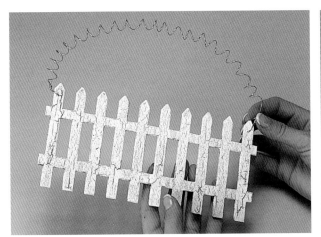

3 Curl the 36" (91cm) piece of gold wire around the wooden dowel. Insert the ends of the wire hanger into the holes of the fence and twist the ends to secure.

4 Tie a bow onto the wire hanger using three strands of natural raffia. Hot glue the wooden birdhouse onto the top left side of the fence, then glue the green moss onto the fence and birdhouse. Glue the miniature ivy sprigs onto the bottom left side of the fence. Glue the three miniature eggs into the bird's nest, then glue the nest onto the fence beside the ivy sprigs. Add the miniature bird to the nest. Next, glue the flowerpot and the shovel. Add a miniature wreath above the flowerpot. Glue the other miniature bird inside the wreath. Add miniature flowers inside the flowerpot and on the fence as desired.

Friendship Makes A Garden Grow!

friendship garden gloves

In just minutes, you can create this cheerful garden accent to brighten a cozy kitchen. For a heart-warming touch, add a special sentiment with a handwritten or printed gift tag. You can customize your gift tag for any occasion such as a birthday (*Sue's Birthday Bouquet*), an anniversary (*Your Love Is In Full Bloom*), or Mother's Day (*Moms Make a Garden Grow*).

materials

- General supplies (see page 6)
- One pair of gardening gloves
- Polyester fiberfill
- Artificial flowers
- 1" (3cm) miniature clay pot
- 2" (5cm) miniature straw hat
- 6" (15cm) pitchfork (you could also use a shovel, hoe or rake)
- 9" (23cm) piece of ⅜"-wide (10mm) green sheer ribbon
- 3" (8cm) artificial dragonfly
- Three 1" (3cm) chenille bumble bees
- 36" (91cm) piece of 18-gauge general purpose wire
- ⅜" (10mm) wooden dowel (to curl wire hanger)
- Five strands of natural raffia

1 Stuff the pair of gloves (including the fingers) with polyester fiberfill. Then hot glue the artificial flowers inside each opening, so that the blooms extend above the gloves.

2 Hot glue the gloves together, with one slightly overlapping the other.

3 Glue the clay pot and three bumble bees in the floral bouquet.

4 Tie a bow with the green ribbon, then glue the bow onto the straw hat. Glue the hat near the center of the gloves. Glue the pitchfork at an angle along the upper brim of the straw hat.

5 Hot glue the dragonfly onto the top right side of the gloves.

6 Curl the 36" (91cm) piece of wire around the wooden dowel, then insert the ends into the top side of each glove for a hanger. Twist the ends of the wire hanger until secure. Tie a bow around the top of the wire hanger using the five strands of natural raffia.

7 Add a gift tag if desired. Attach the tag to the hanger with a ribbon bow.

grapevine bird ball

These two enchanting songbirds have found the perfect place to build their love nest. Nestled in a sunny bouquet of romantic blooms, our feathered friends are ready to sing the sweet melody of spring. This delightful project makes a lovely addition to any sunroom.

materials

- General supplies (see page 6)
- 6" (15cm) grapevine ball
- Green sheet moss
- 20" (51cm) piece of ¼"-wide (6mm) yellow ribbon
- Nine artificial green leaves [approximately 2" (5cm)]
- Yellow and cream artificial flowers
- 2¼" (6cm) bird's nest
- Three 1" (3cm) miniature speckled plastic eggs
- Two 3" (8cm) artificial yellow birds
- 32" (81cm) piece of a 3mm pearl string

1 Tie the 20" (51cm) piece of yellow ribbon into the top of the grapevine ball for a hanger. Knot the ends, then secure the ribbon with hot glue.

2 Hot glue the sheet moss around the top and sides of the grapevine ball.

3 Glue the nine green leaves around the top of the grapevine ball.

4 Glue the three eggs into the nest and accent them with small pieces of moss. Glue the nest on top, in the center of the leaves.

5 Hot glue the floral trims and the two birds onto the grapevine ball.

6 Drape the 32" (81cm) pearl string around the edge of the ball as desired and hot glue it to secure.

keepsake journal

materials: General supplies (see page 6) • 6" x 8" (15cm x 20cm) ivory memory book • 5" x 6½" (13cm x 17cm) torn piece of heavy textured handmade paper with embedded rose petals and leaves • Two artificial green leaves • Small pink or mauve artificial rosebud • Three 3" (8cm) pieces of 3mm ivory pearl string • 2" (5cm) miniature grapevine heart • 8" (20cm) piece of ⅛"-wide (3mm) ivory ribbon

1 Tear the textured handmade paper into a rectangular shape approximately 5" × 6½" (13cm × 16cm). **2** Glue the handmade paper onto the center of the memory album cover using tacky glue or a glue pen. **3** Hot glue the two artificial leaves onto the top left corner. **4** Form a loop with the three pieces of the 3mm ivory string and hot glue them onto the leaves, overlapping each as desired. **5** Hot glue the rosebud onto the pearl strings. **6** Tie a bow with the 8" (20cm) piece of ivory ribbon, then glue the bow onto the top of the miniature grapevine heart. Hot glue the grapevine heart onto the album for the finishing touch.

honey bee garden frame

materials: General supplies (see page 6) • EK Success Ready to Make Frame (approximate dimensions are 5⅝" x 7¼" (14cm x 18cm) with a window size of 3" x 4⅝" (8cm x 12cm) • 1¾" (4cm) split wooden beehive • Delta Ceramcoat acrylic paint: Bright Yellow, Palomino Tan and Spice Brown • Delta Ceramcoat matte interior spray varnish • 12" (30cm) piece of a mini English ivy garland • Three 1" (3cm) chenille bumble bees • Artificial floral trims

1 Basecoat the wooden beehive with Bright Yellow. Apply a second coat of yellow paint, and while it is still wet, blend in some Palomino Tan. Use a liner brush to shade the ridges with Palomino Tan, then Spice Brown. **2** Using an old, worn toothbrush, spatter the beehive with Spice Brown. When dry, apply the matte spray varnish. **3** Hot glue the 12" (30cm) mini ivy garland around the left side and bottom of the frame. **4** Hot glue the wooden beehive just right of the bottom center of the frame. Hot glue the three bees and the floral trims onto the frame. Insert your favorite photo into the frame.

doily bouquet card

materials: General supplies (see page 6) • 5" x 7" (13cm x 18cm) brown corrugated card (folded) • Artificial floral trims (flowers and berry clusters) • Small natural raffia bow • 5" (13cm) round paper doily

1 Fold the sides of the doily inward and overlap to form a cone shape. Glue the overlapping edges to secure. **2** Hot glue the floral trims inside the doily cone. **3** Glue the doily bouquet onto the center of the card. **4** Tie a raffia bow, then hot glue it to the front of the doily bouquet.

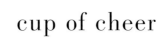

cup of cheer

materials: General supplies (see page 6) • Teacup and saucer with a floral design • Floral foam brick • Assorted floral trims (choose a color scheme to complement the floral design on the teacup and saucer) • 2½" (6cm) miniature jointed bear • 9" (23cm) piece of ⅛"-wide (3mm) ribbon for bow on bear's neck • 12" (30cm) piece of 3mm ivory pearl string

1 Cut a piece of the floral foam to fit inside the teacup. Glue the bottom of the foam piece to the inside of the cup. Insert the stems of the flowers into the floral foam base of the teacup, securing them with hot glue if necessary. **2** Tie the 9" (23cm) piece of ribbon into a bow around the bear's neck. Position the bear in the cup and hot glue it to secure. **3** Hot glue the 12" (30cm) pearl string around the bear and the floral trims. **4** As an option, you can add a printed tag to the handle of the teacup. Your tag could include any special message or sentiment such as *Get Well Soon*, *Thinking of You*, *Happy Birthday* or *Best Wishes*. Cut the tag with decorative edge scissors and add a satin bow. **5** For an elegant finishing touch, you may want to place a round scalloped doily onto the saucer.

garden party

EVERYONE LOVES A GARDEN PARTY! It's the perfect time to celebrate a season of vibrant blooms, fragrant scents, dancing butterflies and the endless beauty Mother Nature bestows upon us. If you lack an outdoor garden setting– don't despair. This chapter is blooming with creative ideas to bring the joy of a magical garden gala indoors.

No garden party is complete without the warm glow of candlelight twinkling in the starlit summer night. From candles trimmed with charming garden accents to an exquisite Floating Candle Centerpiece, you'll find oodles of ideas to add a shimmering touch to your festive celebrations.

And let's not forget the kids! They're guaranteed to go "buggy" over our Gummy Worm Bug Bouquet, the perfect "edible" centerpiece idea. For more creepy critter fun, coordinate the tabletop bug theme with charming Ladybug and Bee Napkin Holders crafted from air-dry clay.

In addition to these great ideas, you'll also find sweet inspiration for fanciful favors to delight your garden party guests. From exquisite Garden Party Crackers and Floral Peat Pot Favors brimming with tasty treats, to whimsical Wiggly Worm Favors for the kids, these party pleasers are sure to capture the hearts of young and old alike.

ladybug and bee
napkin holders

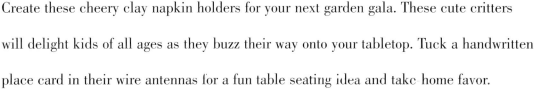

Create these cheery clay napkin holders for your next garden gala. These cute critters will delight kids of all ages as they buzz their way onto your tabletop. Tuck a handwritten place card in their wire antennas for a fun table seating idea and take-home favor.

materials

- Paintbrushes and general supplies (see pages 6–7)
- 1¾" (4cm) wooden napkin rings
- Air-dry modeling clay (I use Creative Paperclay)
- Round wooden toothpicks
- Delta Ceramcoat acrylic paint: Bright Yellow, Charcoal and Light Ivory for the bee, and Cardinal Red, Charcoal and Light Ivory for the ladybug
- Delta Ceramcoat matte interior spray varnish
- 4"x1½" (10cmx4cm) wooden wing cutouts (for bee napkin holders only)
- Two 5" (13cm) pieces of 20-gauge silver wire (for each napkin holder)

tip

For a charming variation of the project, you can glue a magnetic strip onto the back of these fluttering friends for delightful fridge magnets.

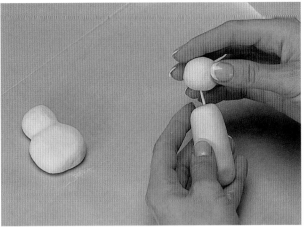

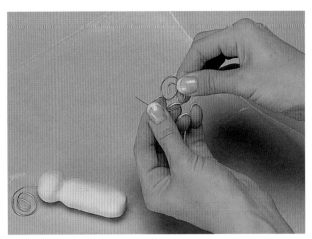

1 For the ladybug, form a 1½" (4cm) ball of the air-dry modeling clay. Then, flatten the ball slightly to form the body of the ladybug. Cut approximately ½" (1cm) off a round wooden toothpick. Insert the remaining toothpick halfway into the top of the clay body. Form a 1" (3cm) ball of clay for the head, then press the ball into the toothpick. Blend the edges of the head onto the body until smooth. For the bee, form another 1½" (4cm) ball of the air-dry modeling clay. Roll the ball of clay into the body shape of the bee, approximately 2" (5cm) long. Follow the directions you used for the ladybug to create the head of the bee.

2 Bend each silver wire piece into a coil shape and insert them into the top of the heads for antennas. Remove the antennas and allow the bugs to dry. When the bugs are dry, apply tacky glue to the bottom of the antennas and insert them back into their holes. Let the glue set.

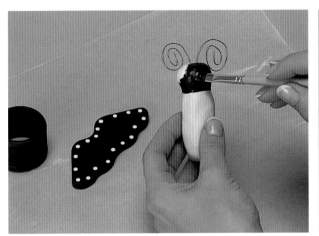

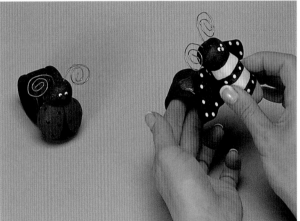

3 Refer to the pattern on page 60 when painting the faces. Basecoat the bee's body with Bright Yellow and the head with Charcoal. Paint the two stripes Charcoal and add Light Ivory dots. Paint the eyes Light Ivory with Charcoal pupils, and paint a Bright Yellow nose. Paint the wooden wings Charcoal with Light Ivory dots around the edge. Basecoat the ladybug's wings with Cardinal Red and the midsection with Charcoal. Paint the dots on the wings Charcoal. Paint the head with Charcoal with eyes that are Light Ivory with Charcoal pupils. Paint the nose Cardinal Red. Paint the wooden napkin rings with Charcoal. Using an old, worn toothbrush, spatter the bugs, wings and wooden napkin rings with Light Ivory. When dry, apply the matte spray varnish.

4 Hot glue the wooden wings onto the back of the bee, and hot glue the wooden napkin rings onto the ladybug and bee.

tip

If slight cracks appear in the Paperclay after drying, just fill them in with more clay and allow the project to dry again.

wiggly worm favors

Look what we found crawling in the garden . . . fashioned from air-dry clay, these wiggly worms look right at home nestled in their mossy peat pot containers. To add a whimsical touch to your miniature worm garden, add a tiny shovel, clay pots and some cheery floral trims. These slithering specimens look adorable peeping through the soil of a potted plant.

materials

FOR THE WORM FAVORS:

- Paintbrushes and general supplies (see pages 6–7)
- Air-dry modeling clay (I use Creative Paperclay)
- Delta Ceramcoat acrylic paint: Seminole Green, Dark Forest Green, Light Ivory, Charcoal and Bright Yellow
- Delta Ceramcoat matte interior spray varnish

FOR THE WORM GARDEN:

- Green sheet moss
- Miniature peat pots, 2½" (6cm) tall
- Artificial floral trims to accent worm garden
- Miniature clay pots (approximately ½" to 1" (1cm to 3cm))
- Miniature shovel approximately 6" (15cm)

tip

You could also add other miniature artificial bugs, such as ladybugs, bees, dragonflies, grasshoppers and butterflies to your garden.

FOR THE WORM FAVORS:

1 Cover your work surface with waxed paper. Form a 1¾" (4cm) ball of the air-dry modeling clay. Roll the ball of clay into a hot dog shape approximately 5" (13cm) long. Use moist fingers to smooth and blend the surface area. Use your fingers to bend the roll of clay into your desired "wiggly" worm shapes and allow to dry.

2 Basecoat the worms with Seminole Green. Paint the stripes Dark Forest Green. Paint the dots by alternating Light Ivory and Bright Yellow. Paint the eyes Light Ivory with Charcoal pupils, and paint the nose Bright Yellow. Using an old, worn toothbrush, spatter the worms with Light Ivory. When dry, apply the matte spray varnish.

FOR THE WORM GARDEN:

3 Hot glue pieces of sheet moss into the peat pots.

4 Place your wiggly worms into the moss, so it looks like the worms are coming out of the ground. Don't glue the worms into the pots if you want to use them as take-home gifts. You can hot glue the worms if you plan to use your worm garden as a permanent decoration.

5 Accent your worm garden with the floral trims and miniature clay pots. For the final touch, add a miniature shovel to "dig out" the worms. Hot glue the embellishments in place if desired.

floating candle centerpiece

Add a warm glow to your tabletop décor with this exquisite floating candle centerpiece. Nestled in a charming garden wreath, a small metal bucket provides an unusual backdrop for your flickering flames. The decorated wreath also makes an enchanting keepsake to brighten your wall or doorway.

materials

- General supplies (see page 6)
- Metal pail (approximately 5½" (14cm) high)
- 10" (25cm) grapevine wreath (be sure the inside diameter of the wreath is large enough for the pail)
- Artificial ivy garland (approximately 48" (122cm) in length)
- Three clusters of artificial flowers with leaves and berries
- Three 1"x1¼" (3cmx3cm) miniature clay pots
- Three miniature garden tools approximately 6" (15cm) long (I use one shovel and two hoes)
- 2" (5cm) miniature straw hat
- Miniature artificial insects (I use two dragonflies, one grasshopper, one butterfly and one bumble bee)
- Three floating candles

1 Wrap the 48" (122cm) garland around the wreath, then hot glue it to secure.

2 Hot glue the three clusters of floral trims spaced evenly around the wreath.

3 Glue the miniature clay pots and the garden tools onto the wreath.

4 Glue the straw hat and the artificial insects onto the wreath, saving one of the dragonflies to glue to the front of the pail.

5 Set the pail inside the wreath. Glue the remaining dragonfly to the front of the pail.

6 Fill the pail with water, then add the three floating candles.

tips

Sprinkle real or artificial flower petals onto the surface of the water for a romantic touch.

Look for floating candles with a garden theme such as leaves, flowers, frogs or insects.

You can use the centerpiece as a magic garden wishing well. Just throw in a penny and make a special wish.

The project easily adapts to an autumn centerpiece. Simply use harvest-themed accents such as fall leaves, miniature scarecrows, artificial pumpkins, gourds, golden sunflowers and acorns. Look for fall-themed floating candles in such shapes as pumpkins, fall leaves and apples.

floral birdhouse centerpiece

A papier mâché birdhouse becomes an enchanting centerpiece when painted and accented with a blooming bouquet of floral delights. A charming array of miniature garden trims adds the perfect finishing touch to your storybook cottage. In keeping with the bird theme, accent each dinner plate with a small artificial bird's nest filled with egg-shaped chocolates, almonds or jelly beans.

materials

- Paintbrushes and general supplies (see page 6)
- Papier mâché birdhouse [approximately 6½" x 7" (17cm x 18cm)]
- Delta Ceramcoat acrylic paint: Light Ivory, Dark Forest Green and Burnt Umber
- Delta Ceramcoat matte interior spray varnish
- Floral trims in pink, mauve, ivory and green (I use artificial flowers, leaves, ivy foliage, paper rosebuds and berry clusters)
- 1½" (4cm) miniature bird's nest
- Three ½" (1cm) plastic speckled eggs
- Two 1½" (4cm) miniature mauve or pink birds
- 2" (5cm) miniature grapevine wreath
- ½" (1cm) miniature clay pot

1   Basecoat the birdhouse Light Ivory with a Dark Forest Green rooftop and base.

2   Antique the birdhouse with a wash of Burnt Umber, then use an old, worn toothbrush to spatter the birdhouse with Burnt Umber and Light Ivory.

3   Apply the matte spray varnish.

4   Hot glue the floral trims onto the left side of the house, beginning at the base and extending up to the rooftop. Begin by gluing the larger leaves, ivy foliage and flowers, then accent with the smaller rosebuds and berry clusters.

5   Hot glue the three miniature eggs inside the nest, then glue the nest onto the floral trims.

6   Hot glue the two miniature birds, one beside the nest and the other onto the floral trims at the center of the base.

7   For the final touch, hot glue the miniature wreath and clay pot at the edge of the floral trims near the right edge of the base.

golden glow
candle jar

With just a few paints and garden trims, you can recycle those glass mason jars into delightful candleholders and add a golden garden glow to your patio décor.

materials

- Paintbrushes and general supplies (see page 6)
- Mason jar
- Small pieces of sponge
- Delta Ceramcoat acrylic paint: Palomino Tan, Seminole Green, Light Ivory, Metallic Kim Gold
- Delta Ceramcoat matte interior spray varnish
- 13" (33cm) piece of 1⅜"-wide (3cm) green plaid ribbon
- Tacky glue or Fabri-Tac permanent adhesive
- Artificial floral trims (white daisies, berry clusters and green leaves)
- 10" (25cm) piece of mini artificial ivy garland
- 10" (25cm) piece of ⅜"-wide (10mm) sheer green ribbon
- 8" (20cm) piece of ⅛"-wide (3mm) yellow ribbon
- Chenille bumble bee
- Glass votive candleholder (to fit inside opening of jar) and candle

1 Use a small piece of dampened sponge to basecoat the jar with Palomino Tan. Apply several coats to ensure solid coverage.

2 When dry, sponge paint the jar sparingly with Seminole Green then Metallic Kim Gold for texture. Allow the paint to dry between coats.

3 Use an old, worn toothbrush to spatter the jar with Light Ivory. When dry, apply the matte spray varnish.

4 Use permanent adhesive or tacky glue to secure the 13" (33cm) piece of the green plaid ribbon around the center of the jar.

5 Hot glue the green leaves, white daisies and berry clusters onto the ribbon. For a stronger visual effect, glue the trims in separate bunches or clusters evenly spaced around the jar.

6 Hot glue the 10" (25cm) piece of mini ivy garland around the top of the jar.

7 Tie bows with the 10" (25cm) piece of the ⅜" (10mm) green ribbon and the 8" (20cm) piece of the ⅛" (3mm) yellow ribbon. Hot glue the green bow onto the top right side of one of the daisy clusters, then glue the yellow bow onto the center of the green bow.

8 Hot glue the bumble bee just above the two bows.

9 Set the glass votive candleholder and candle in the jar.

tip

All measurements are based on a standard size mason jar. Since jars may vary in size, it's best to check measurements before you start your project.

gummy worm bug bouquet

Kids love all kinds of creepy, crawly critters . . . especially when they're sweet and tasty! And this "edible" centerpiece idea will make them squeal with delight. Simply place your decorated bug pot onto a glass pedestal plate sprinkled with gummy worms and chocolate cookie crumb "dirt." Add extra fun to your "going buggy" party theme with the Ladybug and Bee Napkin Holders on page 48 and our whimsical Wiggly Worm Favors on page 50.

materials

- General supplies (see page 6)
- 2½" (6cm) rose pot [4" (10cm) high]
- Floral foam brick
- Green sheet moss
- Floral roping garland [approximately 10½" (27cm)] or desired floral trims to accent pot
- Green floral wire or general purpose wire (for bug stems)
- Artificial bugs (I use three wooden ladybugs, two butterflies, one bee, one grasshopper and one dragonfly)
- Glass serving or pedestal plate
- Chocolate cookie crumbs
- Gummy worms, sugared worm candies and any other edible bugs you can find

1 Cut a piece of the floral foam brick to fit inside the clay pot. Apply a generous amount of hot glue onto the bottom of the foam piece and insert it into the pot.

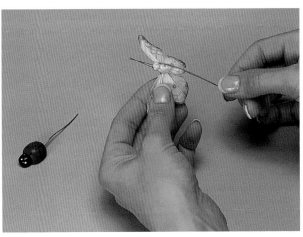

2 Cut pieces of wire to various lengths, approximately 2" to 3" (5cm to 8cm), for the bug stems. Hot glue the wire stems onto the bugs and allow the glue to set.

3 Insert the wire stems of the bugs into the floral foam base of the pot. Position the bugs at various heights and angles, then hot glue small pieces of moss at the base to conceal the foam. Hot glue the 10½" (27cm) garland around the base of the pot. Instead of the floral garland, you can use miniature floral trims to accent the pot.

4 Set the bug bouquet in the center of a glass serving plate. Sprinkle chocolate cookie crumbs onto the plate (for dirt) and add gummy worms, sugared worm candies and any other edible bugs you can "dig up!"

tip

For a "sweet" centerpiece idea, you could decorate the plate with some "creepy cupcakes" topped with cookie crumb dirt and yummy gummy worms or other varieties of candy bugs.

garden party crackers

· ·

materials: General supplies (see page 6) • 5½" (14cm) long card-board tubes (I cut a paper towel roll in half) • 12"x12" (30cmx30cm) pieces of tissue paper • ⅛"-wide (3mm) ivory ribbon • Floral and garden-themed trims and embellishments • Treats to place inside the cracker favors

1 Place the 5½" (14cm) cardboard tube along the bottom center of a 12"×12" (30cm×30cm) piece of tissue paper for each favor. Roll the tube tightly along the full length of the tissue, then secure the overlapping edge with glue. **2** Place the treats inside the tube, then tie each end with a piece of the ⅛" (3mm) ivory ribbon. You could also tie the edges with curling rib-bon, raffia or twine. **3** Hot glue the floral and garden-themed trims to the top of the party crackers. For these designs, I embellished with: floral trims accented with a 6" (15cm) 3mm ivory pearl string on each side, a 2" (5cm) miniature grapevine wreath accented with floral trims, and two artificial leaves with a 1½" (4cm) miniature bird's nest and three ½" (1cm) eggs glued inside.

tip These party crackers make great favors for a garden-themed wedding or bridal shower.

romantic butterfly candle

· ·

materials: Paintbrushes and general supplies (see page 6) • 4" (10cm) pillar candle • Clay pot saucer [5" (13cm) diameter] • Delta Ceramcoat acrylic paint: Spice Brown, Light Ivory and Metallic Kim Gold • Delta Ceramcoat matte interior spray varnish • Small piece of sponge • Green sheet moss • 2½" (6cm) artificial pink butterfly • 10" (25cm) piece of ¼"-wide (6mm) pink ribbon • Floral trims

1 Basecoat the clay pot saucer with Spice Brown. When dry, use a small piece of dampened sponge to apply Light Ivory then Metallic Kim Gold. Allow the paint to dry in between coats. **2** Apply the matte spray varnish to the saucer. **3** Set the candle inside the saucer. Hot glue the green sheet moss around the entire edge of the saucer. **4** Hot glue the floral trims onto the moss. Hot glue the butterfly onto the floral trims. **5** Tie a bow with the 10" (25cm) piece of the pink ribbon. Hot glue the bow onto the edge of the saucer, just beneath the butterfly.

floral peat pot favors

materials: General supplies (see page 6) • Peat pots (3" (8cm) diameter) • Delta Ceramcoat acrylic paint: Light Ivory, Seminole Green and Metallic Kim Gold • Delta Ceramcoat matte interior spray varnish • Small piece of sponge • 24" (61cm) piece of 20-gauge gold wire for each hanger • 3/8" (10mm) wooden dowel • Floral trims • 7" (18cm) piece of 1/8"-wide (3mm) gold ribbon (for each bow) • Treats or favors

1 Using a small piece of dampened sponge, basecoat the outside of the pots with Light Ivory. Apply several coats to ensure solid coverage. **2** When dry, sponge paint the pots with Seminole Green, then Metallic Kim Gold for texture. Allow the paint to dry between coats, then apply the matte spray varnish. **3** Curl the 24" (61cm) piece of the gold wire around the wooden dowel. Insert each end of the wire into the top sides of the pot. Twist the ends of the wire to secure. **4** Hot glue floral trims to the front of the pot. **5** For each pot, tie a bow with a 7" (18cm) piece of the gold ribbon. Hot glue the bow onto the pot to accent the floral trims. **6** Fill the pot with the treats or small favors. If you like, you can add natural excelsior or paper shredding into the bottom of each pot first. For a personal touch, add a name tag to each pot with a curling ribbon.

garden gate candle

materials: Paintbrushes and general supplies (see page 6) • 4" (10cm) pillar candle • Clay pot saucer (5" (13cm) diameter) • Delta Ceramcoat acrylic paint: Spice Brown, Georgia Clay, Light Ivory and Metallic Kim Gold • Delta Ceramcoat matte interior spray varnish • Small piece of sponge • Green sheet moss • Miniature wooden wired fence • Three wooden flower pot splits (1" x 1 1/8" (3cm x 3cm)) • General purpose wire • Garden embellishments (such as mini English ivy garland, artificial green berries, miniature birds, watering can, 1/2" (1cm) miniature eggs, floral trims and a dragonfly)

1 Basecoat the clay pot saucer with Spice Brown. When dry, use a small piece of dampened sponge to apply Light Ivory, then Metallic Kim Gold. Allow the paint to dry between coats. Paint the three wooden flowerpots with Georgia Clay. **2** Cut a piece of the wooden fence long enough to fit around the diameter of the candle. Paint the fence with Light Ivory. Apply the matte spray varnish to the saucer, fence and flowerpots. **3** Attach the wooden fence around the base of the candle using a small piece of general purpose wire. Twist the ends of the wire to secure. **4** Hot glue the three wooden flowerpots around the fence. Glue moss inside each of the pots. **5** Set the candle inside the saucer. Hot glue the green sheet moss around the edge of the saucer and to accent the fence. **6** Hot glue the garden embellishments around the saucer, onto the fence and inside the clay pots as desired.

using patterns & templates

using patterns & templates

The project patterns are featured on pages 59-61. You can transfer these patterns using tracing and transfer paper, or you can trace them freehand, using the pattern as a visual reference.

transferring patterns

Use a pencil to trace the desired pattern onto a sheet of transparent tracing paper. Insert a piece of gray transfer paper in between the traced pattern and your surface area. Using a pencil or ballpoint pen, retrace the pattern, transferring it to your surface. Since the transfer paper is coated on one side only, be sure the correct side is facing down by making a small mark to test. To make transferring easier, use masking tape to secure the tracing and transfer paper.

tip

Do not transfer the cheek areas. They were drawn on the patterns for visual reference only. Since the cheeks are softly drybrushed, it may be difficult to cover the line left if the cheek area is transferred or sketched.

TRACE THE PATTERN ONTO THE SURFACE USING TRANSFER PAPER.

painting details

You can transfer the finer details of your projects using the patterns. Just remember to basecoat all areas first. For the simpler projects, instead of transferring the finer details using the tracing and transfer paper method, you can draw them freehand with a pencil using the pattern or finished project photo as a visual reference.

creating templates

When making the kraft paper projects, such as Lilly Ladybug (see page 12) or the Paper Bag Garden Angel (see page 28), I find it easier to create a permanent template first. Instead of transferring each shape directly onto the kraft paper, transfer the shape onto a piece of lightweight cardboard or posterboard to make a cardboard template. You can use this template over and over again simply by tracing around the outer edges with a pencil. This technique will save you lots of time, especially if you plan to make several projects requiring the same basic shape.

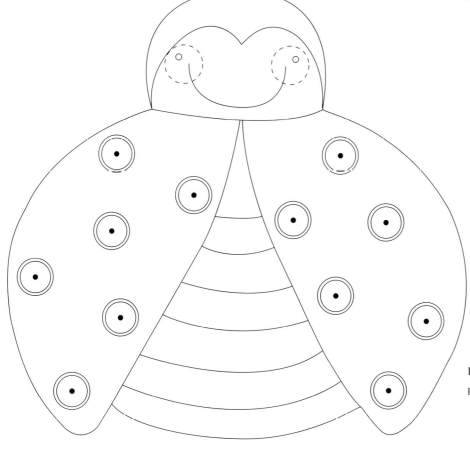

Lilly Ladybug, page 12. Enlarge this pattern to 182% to bring to full size.

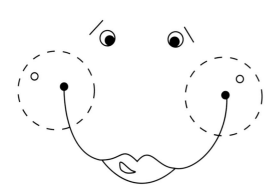

Madame Butterfly, page 27, and Flower Fairy Keepsake Box, page 24.

Glass Ball Bunny Ornament, page 21.

patterns

Bloomin' Bugs, page 17.

Ladybug and Bee Napkin
Holders and Wiggly Worm
Favors, pages 48 and 50.

Paper Bag Garden Angel, page 28. Enlarge this
pattern to 154% to bring to full size.

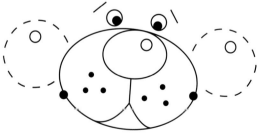

Bumble Bee Bear, page 14.

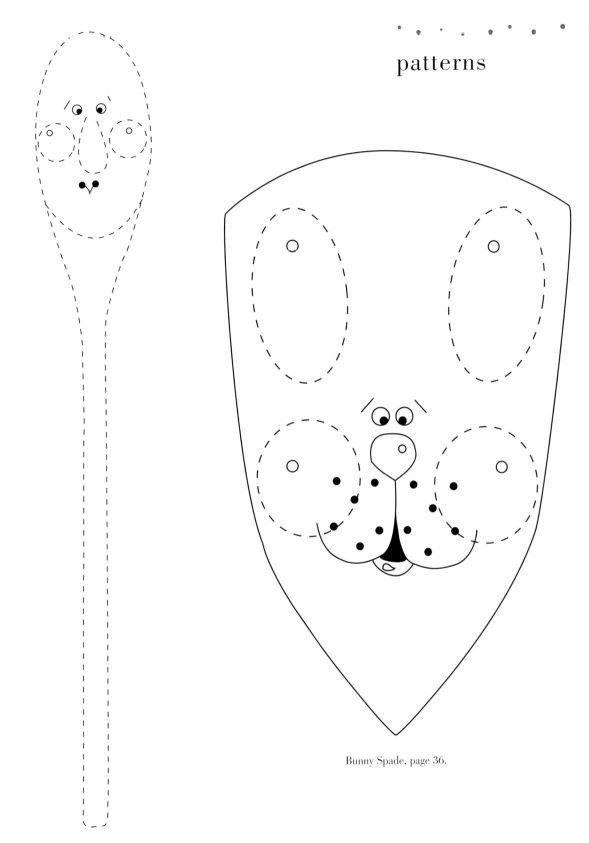

Bunny Spade, page 36.

Spoon Fairy, page 30. Enlarge this pattern to 143% to bring to full size. Note: the size of the spoon will vary.

resources

Activa Products, Inc.

512 S. Garrett
Marshall, TX 75670
(903) 938-2224
www.activa-products.com
• Celluclay Instant Papier Mâché

Creative Paperclay Company, Inc.

79 Daily Dr., Ste. 101
Camarillo, CA 93010
(805) 484-6648
www.paperclay.com
• Creative Paperclay air-dry modeling compound

Delta Technical Coatings, Inc.

2550 Pellissier Pl.
Whittier, CA 90601
(800) 423-4135
www.deltacrafts.com
• Delta Ceramcoat acrylic paints, matte interior spray varnish, gesso, crackle medium and general painting supplies

Duncan Enterprises, Inc.

5673 E. Shields Ave.
Fresno, CA 93727
(800) 438-6226 or (559) 291-4444
E-mail: consumer@duncanmail.com
www.duncancrafts.com
• Tulip Dimensional Paints

FloraCraft (Dow Styrofoam)

One Longfellow Place
P.O. Box 400
Ludington, MI 49431
(800) 253-0409
E-mail. postmasterl@floracraft.com
www.floracraft.com
www.styrofoamcrafts.com
• Styrofoam brand plastic foam products

Loew-Cornell, Inc.

563 Chestnut Ave.
Teaneck, NJ 07666-2491
(201) 836-7070
E-mail: loew-cornell@loew-cornell.com
www.loew-cornell.com
• Paintbrushes and general painting supplies